CW00925436

Robert Burns
Nature
Poems

First published in Great Britain in 2025 by Pyramid, an imprint of
Octopus Publishing Group Ltd
Carmelite House
50 Victoria Embankment
London EC4Y 0DZ
www.octopusbooks.co.uk

An Hachette UK Company
www.hachette.co.uk

The authorized representative in the EEA is Hachette Ireland,
8 Castlecourt Centre, Dublin 15, D15 XTP3, Ireland (email: info@hbgi.ie)

Distributed in the US by Hachette Book Group
1290 Avenue of the Americas, 4th and 5th Floors
New York, NY 10104

Distributed in Canada by Canadian Manda Group
664 Annette St., Toronto, Ontario, Canada M6S 2C8

ISBN 978-0-7537-3558-9

A CIP catalogue record for this book is available from the British Library.

Printed and bound in Great Britain.

10 9 8 7 6 5 4 3 2 1

Publisher: Lucy Pessell
Editor: Tim Leng
Designer: Isobel Platt
Assistant Editor: Samina Rahman
Production Controller: Sarah Parry

Compiling Editor: Robert Tuesley Anderson
Illustrations by The Ink Bothy

Robert Burns
Nature Poems

A Poet's Grace

O You, who kindly does provide
For every creature's want!
We bless the God of Nature wide
For all Your goodness lent.
And if it please You, heavenly Guide,
May never worse be sent;
But, whether granted or denied,
Lord, bless us with content.

O You, in whom we live and move,
Who made the sea and shore,
Your goodness constantly we prove,
And, grateful, would adore;
And, if it please You, Power above!
Still grant us with such store
The friend we trust, the fair we love,
And we desire no more.

Contents

Introduction

Scotland's national poet Robert ('Rabbie') Burns was born in Alloway, Ayrshire, on 25 January 1759, the son of an impoverished tenant farmer. Like his father, Burns would spend much of his life trying to eke out a living from the land, first in Ayrshire and later in Dumfriesshire, both in south-east Scotland. Only later in life, while living in the town of Dumfries with his wife, Jean Armour, and his large family and working as an exciseman, was he able, for a time, to establish a more settled life, although one marred by ill health and fits of despondency. He died on 21 July 1796, aged just 37.

'Heaven-taught ploughman'

Burns began writing poetry in his youth, usually writing in Scots (a sister language of English) or Scottish English, or in a blend of both, and published his first collection, *Poems, Chiefly in the Scots Dialect*, in 1786, in the Ayrshire town of Kilmarnock. His poems, which include some of his most celebrated such as 'To a Louse' and 'The Cotter's Saturday Night', won Burns both popular and critical success. This led him to settle for some 14 months in Edinburgh, where he was feted as an untutored 'poet of the people' – a 'heaven-taught ploughman', in the words of one contemporary critic. In reality, however, the largely self-educated Burns had a cosmopolitan knowledge of literature, including Latin and French as well as Scots and English, and as a poet he was always a consummate, meticulous craftsman.

In the Scottish capital, Burns sat for his portrait with Alexander Nasmyth (now in the Scottish National Portrait

Gallery) and oversaw the publication of a new, expanded edition of his poems (published 1787). He also began work on the project that was to consume much of his free time for the rest of his life – the research and recreation of traditional Scottish songs for James Johnson's *The Scots Musical Museum* (1787–1803) and George Thomson's *A Select Collection of Original Scottish Airs for the Voice* (1793–1818). To these collections belong some of Burns best-loved songs such as 'Auld Lang Syne' and 'A Red, Red Rose'. His lively but unsettling stay in Edinburgh also inspired him to write, after he left the city, his most ambitious work, the narrative poem 'Tam O'Shanter', the comic story of a drunken farmer's encounter with revelling witches and warlocks in an Ayrshire kirk (church).

After his death, Burns's reputation as Scotland's greatest poetic genius grew apace, his commemoration taking on near cult-like status. His friends held the first Burns Supper in 1801 (first on the anniversary of his death and, in the following year, on his birthday) – which has remained an institution in Scotland and the Scottish diaspora ever since. At the same time, too, Burns Clubs were set up to celebrate the poet's life, works and home country.

Nature – the bedrock of Burns's poetry

Burns's poetry covers a wide variety of subject matter – love won and lost, the vicissitudes of farm life, the injustices faced by the poor, Scottish patriotism, and satires on religion and politics – but the Scottish countryside is an enduring motif that appears across many of his works. His graft as a young farm labourer and later his journeys on horseback through the riverscapes, hills and farmlands of south-west Scotland gave him an intimate knowledge of nature through every season – whether driech, stormy winters or short, uncertain summers. Reading his poetry, especially his depictions of the sourer weathers, has an almost immersive effect: we can feel the rain, dark and cold with Tam O'Shanter as he journeys through the night in a late-autumn storm. Burns's intimacy with nature also gave him a deep sympathy with the creatures – the 'wee, sleekit, cowrin, tim'rous beasties' – he daily encountered, whether his own horses, his dogs or the eponymous mouse found in a field in one of his most famous poems. For Burns, humans and animals were 'earth-born companions'.

Love and nature go hand and hand in Burns's poetry. Lovemaking takes place in the fields, woods and rivers of rural Scotland, and spring and summer above all are associated with the joys of love, autumn and winter with its woes. Burns's love poems reflect not only his own experience – he was something of a 'ladies' man', especially in his youth – but also his self-conscious adoption of a long poetic tradition of pastoral love poetry dating back to classical times – from poets such as the 3rd-century BCE Greek Theocritus, through the 15th-century Scottish makar (court poet) Robert Henryson and, of course, William Shakespeare, to his immediate Scottish predecessors, such as the Edinburgh poet Robert Fergusson.

For all of the uncertainty of its weather and the hardships suffered by ordinary working people, Burns's depiction of his native country is always shot through with a sense of pride and nostalgia for its wild and generous beauty. For Burns, the rivers of southern Scotland – the Ayr, the Nith and the Tweed, among them – are just as majestic and worthy of celebration as the great rivers of the poetic canon – the Tiber, the Thames, the Loire – and the humble hills of his neighbourhood as great a source of inspiration as Parnassus, the Greek mountain sacred to Apollo and the Muses. The landscapes of Scotland were the enduring bedrock of his poetry and his politics.

Robert Tuesley Anderson

Robert Tuesley Anderson is an author and poet living near Jedburgh, in the Scottish Borders, a town where Burns briefly resided in 1787 and was presented with the freedom of the royal burgh. While not Scottish born and bred, he has long made Scotland his home, has fallen in love with its landscapes and its poetry, and has even dared to preside over a Burns Supper or two.

The Ink Bothy

Isobel Buchanan is a printmaker and illustrator based in rural Aberdeenshire. She specializes in linocut, drawing on Scottish historic sites, the Isles, the Ocean and wild rugged landscapes, iconic geology and wildlife. Her work is bold and textured, primarily black and white, often incorporating dynamic abstract and semi-abstract designs. Instagram: @theinkbothy

Timorous Beasties

Address to
the Woodlark

O, stay, sweet warbling woodlark, stay,
Nor quit for me the trembling spray!
A hapless lover courts your lay,
Your soothing, fond complaining.

Again, again that tender part,
That I may catch your melting art!
For surely that would touch her heart,
Who kills me with disdaining.

Say, was your little mate unkind,
And heard you as the careless wind?
O, nothing but love and sorrow joined
Such notes of woe could waken!

You tell of never-ending care,
Of speechless grief and dark despair –
For pity's sake, sweet bird, no more,
Or my poor heart is broken!

The Old Farmer's
New-Year Morning Salutation
to His Old Mare, Maggie.

On giving her the accustomed handful of
corn to handsel in the new year.

A Good New Year I wish thee, Maggie!
Hae, there is a handful from the sheaf to your old belly:
Though, you are hollow backed now, and knobby,
I have seen the day
You could have gone like any colt,
Out over the lea.

Although now you are drooping, stiff, and crazy,
And your old hide as white as a daisy,
I have seen you dappled, sleek and shiny,
A bonny grey:
He should been prepared that dared to excite you,
Once in a day.

You once was in the foremost rank,
A filly stately, compact, and limber:
And set well down a shapely shank
As ever tread earth;
And could have flown out over a moat
Like any bird.

It is now some nine-and-twenty year
Since you was my father-in-law's mare;
He gave me you, wholly as a dowry,
And fifty mark;
Though it was small, it was well won wealth,
And you was strong.

When first I went to court my Jenny,
You then was trotting with your mother:
Though you was tricky, sly, and funny,
You never was mischievous;
But homely, tractable, quiet, and pleasant,
And uncommonly good tempered.

That day, you pranced with much pride,
When you bore home my lovely bride:
And sweet and graceful she did ride,
With maiden air!
Kyle-Stewart I could have challenged wide,
For such a pair.

Though now you can but stumble and hobble,
And stagger like a salmon boat,
That day, you was a goer noble,
For heels and wind!
And ran them till they all did wobble,
Far, far behind!

When you and I were young and skittish,
And stable-meals at fairs were tedious,
How you would prance, and snort, and whinny,
And take the road!
Town's people ran, and stood aloof,
And called you mad.

When you was fed with corn, and I was mellow,
We took the road yes like a swallow:
At wedding races you had never a fellow,
For pith and speed;
But every tail you paid them hollow,
Wherever you went.

...

The small, short rumped, hunter cattle
Might sometimes have beat you for a spurt;
But six Scotch miles you tried their mettle,
And made them wheeze:
No whip nor spur, but just a twig
Of willow or hazel.

You were a noble near horse to the plough,
As ever in tug or tow was drawn!
Often you and I, in eight hours going,
On good March weather,
Have turned six rods by our own hand
For days together.

You never pulled rashly, stopped sudden, or capered.
But your old tail you would have whisked,
And spread abroad your well filled breast,
With vigour and power,
Till rooty hillocks would have roared, and cracked,
And fallen smoothly over.

When frosts lay long, and snows were deep,
And threatened labour back to keep,
I gave your dish a small bit heap
Above the edge:
I knew my Maggie would not sleep
For that, ere summer.

In cart or car you never refused to go;
The stiffest incline you would have faced it;
You never leaped, and sprang, and sprung forward,
Then stood to blow;
But just your step a little slower,
You jogged along.

My plough team is now your issue all,
Four gallant brutes as ever did pull;
As well as six more I have sold away,
That you have nursed;
They drew me thirteen pounds and two,
The very worst.

Many a sore day's we two have worked,
And with the weary world fought!
And many an anxious day I thought
We would be beat!
Yet here to crazy age we are brought,
With something yet.

And think not, my old trusty servant,
That now perhaps you are less deserving,
And your old days may end in starving;
For my last bushel,
A heaped quarter-peck, I will reserve one
Laid by for you.

We have worn to crazy years together;
We will totter about with one another;
With attentive care I will change your tether
To some reserved patch,
Where you may nobly stretch your stomach
With small fatigue.

To a Louse

On seeing one on a lady's bonnet
at church.

Ha! Where are you going, you crawling wonder?
Your impudence protects you sorely,
I can not say but you swagger rarely
Over gauze and lace,
Though faith! I fear you dine but sparingly
On such a place

You ugly, creeping, blasted wonder,
Detested, shunned by saint and sinner,
How dare you set your foot upon her –
Such fine a lady!
Go somewhere else and seek your dinner
On some poor body

Off! in some beggar's temples squat:
There you may creep, and sprawl, and scramble,
With other kindred, jumping cattle,
In shoals and nations;
Where horn nor bone never dare unsettle
Your thick plantations

Now hold you there! you are out of sight,
Below the falderals, snug and tight;
No, faith you yet! you will not be right,
Until you have got on it –
The very topmost, towering height
Of miss's bonnet.

My sooth! right bold you set your nose out,
  As plump and grey as any gooseberry:
    O for some rank, mercurial resin,
      Or deadly, red powder,
I would give you such a hearty dose of it,
      Would dress your breech!

  I would not have been surprised to spy
    You on an old wife's flannel cap:
    Or maybe some small ragged boy,
        On his undervest;
    But Miss's fine balloon bonnet! fye!
        How dare you do it.

      O Jenny do not toss your head,
    And set your beauties all abroad!
    You little know what cursed speed
        The blastie's making!
  Those winks and finger-ends, I dread,
        Are notice taking!

  O would some Power the gift to give us
    To see ourselves as others see us!
  It would from many a blunder free us,
        And foolish notion:
What airs in dress and gait would leave us,
        And even devotion!

From: The Two Dogs

A Tale

It was in that place of Scotland's isle,
That bears the name of old King Coil,
Upon a lovely day in June,
When wearing through the afternoon,
Two dogs, that were not busy at home,
Chance-met once upon a time.
The first I'll name, they called him Caesar,
Was kept for 'his Honor's' pleasure:
His hair, his size, his mouth, his ears,
Showed he was none of Scotland's dogs;
But bred some place far abroad,
Where sailors go to fish for cod.
His locked, lettered, lovely brass collar
Showed him the gentleman and scholar;
But although he was of high degree,
The fiend of pride, no pride had he;
But would have spent an hour caressing,
Even with a tinker-gypsy's mongrel;
At church or market, mill or smithy,
No matted cur, though ever so ragged,
But he would have stood, as glad to see him,
And pissed on stones and hillocks with him.
The other was a ploughman's collie,
A rhyming, ranting, raving rollicking young friend,
Who for his friend and comrade had him,
And in his youth had Luath named him,
After some dog in Highland song,
Was made long past – Lord knows how long.

He was a wise and faithful cur,
As ever leaped a ditch or stone fence.
His honest, pleasant, white streaked face
Always got him friends in every place;
His breast was white, his shaggy back
Well clad with coat of glossy black;
His joyous tail, with upward curl,
Hung over his buttocks with a swirl.

Sonnet on Hearing
a Thrush Sing

Sing on, sweet thrush, upon the leafless bough,
Sing on, sweet bird, I listen to thy strain,
See aged Winter, 'mid his surly reign,
At thy blithe carol, clears his furrowed brow.
Thus in bleak Poverty's dominion drear,
Sits meek Content with light, unanxious heart;
Welcomes the rapid moments, bids them part,
Nor asks if they bring ought to hope or fear.
I thank thee, Author of this opening day!
Thou whose bright sun now gilds yon orient skies!
Riches denied, thy boon was purer joys –
What wealth could never give nor take away!
But come, thou child of poverty and care,
The mite high heav'n bestow'd, that mite with thee I'll share.

On Seeing
a Wounded Hare
Limp by Me
Which a Fellow
Had Just Shot At

Inhuman man! curse on your barbarous art,
And blasted be your murder-aiming eye;
May never pity soothe you with a sigh,
Nor never pleasure glad your cruel heart!

Go live, poor wanderer of the wood and field,
The bitter little that of life remains!
No more the thickening brackens and verdant plains
To you shall home, or food, or pastime yield.

Seek, mangled wretch, some place of accustomed rest,
No more of rest, but now your dying bed!
The sheltering rushes whistling over your head,
The cold earth with your bloody bosom pressed.

Often as by winding Nith I musing, wait
The sober evening, or hail the cheerful dawn,
I will miss you sporting over the dewy lawn,
And curse the ruffian's aim, and mourn your hapless fate.

From: Tam O'Shanter

Tam and his grey mare Maggie
are fleeing from the witches.

Now, do your speedy utmost, Meg,
And win the key-stone of the brig;
There, at them you your tail may toss,
A running stream they dare not cross!
But before the key-stone she could make,
The fiend a tail she had to shake;
For Nannie, far before the rest,
Hard upon noble Maggie pressed,
And flew at Tam with furious aim;
But little was she Maggie's mettle!
One spring brought off her master whole,
But left behind her own grey tail:
The old woman clutched her by the rump,
And left poor Maggie scarce a stump.

To a Mouse

On turning her up in her nest with the plough,
November 1785.

Small, sleek, cowering, timorous beast,
O, what a panic is in your breast!
You need not start away so hasty
With hurrying scamper!
I would be loath to run and chase you,
With murdering plough-staff.

I'm truly sorry man's dominion
Has broken Nature's social union,
And justifies that ill opinion
Which makes thee startle
At me, thy poor, earth born companion
And fellow mortal!

I doubt not, sometimes, but you may steal;
What then? Poor beast, you must live!
An odd ear in twenty-four sheaves
Is a small request;
I will get a blessing with what is left,
And never miss it.

Your small house, too, in ruin!
It's feeble walls the winds are scattering!
And nothing now, to build a new one,
Of coarse grass green!
And bleak December's winds coming,
Both bitter and keen!

You saw the fields laid bare and wasted,
And weary winter coming fast,
And cozy here, beneath the blast,
You thought to dwell,
Till crash! the cruel plough past
Out through your cell.

That small bit heap of leaves and stubble,
Has cost you many a weary nibble!
Now you are turned out, for all your trouble,
Without house or holding,
To endure the winter's sleety dribble,
And hoar-frost cold.

But Mouse, you are not alone,
In proving foresight may be vain:
The best laid schemes of mice and men
Go often askew,
And leaves us nothing but grief and pain,
For promised joy!

Still you are blest, compared with me!
The present only touches you:
But oh! I backward cast my eye,
On prospects dreary!
And forward, though I cannot see,
I guess and fear!

A Mother's Lament

Fate gave the word – the arrow sped,
And pierced my darling's heart,
And with him all the joys are fled
Life can to me impart.
By cruel hands the sapling drops,
In dust dishonoured laid:
So fell the pride of all my hopes,
My age's future shade.

The mother linnet in the brake
Bewails her ravished young:
So I for my lost darling's sake
Lament the live-day long.
Death, often I have feared your fatal blow!
Now fond I bare my breast!
O, do you kindly lay me low,
With him I love at rest!

The Wren's Nest

The Robin cam to the wren's nest
And keekit in and keekit in,
O weel's me on your auld pow,
Wad ye be in, wad ye be in.
Ye'se ne'er get leave to lie without,
And I within, and I within,
As lang's I hae an auld clout
To row you in, to row you in.

Trees,
Flowers
and Grains

The Primrose

Do you ask me, why I send you here
The firstling of the infant year:
This lovely native of the vale,
That hangs so pensive and so pale?

Look on its bending stalk, so weak.
That, each way yielding, does not break,
And see how aptly it reveals
The doubts and fears a lover feels.

Look on its leaves of yellow hue
Bepearled thus with morning dew,
And these will whisper in your ears:–
'The sweets of loves are washed with tears.'

Fine Flowers in the Valley

She sat down below a thorn,
Fine flowers in the valley,
And there she has her sweet babe born
And the green leaves they grow rarely.

Smile not so sweet, my lovely babe
Fine flowers in the valley,
And you smile so sweet, you will smile me dead
And the green leaves they grow rarely.

She has taken out her little penknife
Fine flowers in the valley,
And robbed the sweet babe of its life,
And the green leaves they grow rarely.

She has dug a grave by the light of the moon,
Fine flowers in the valley,
And there she has buried her sweet babe in,
And the green leaves they grow rarely.

As she was going to the church,
Fine flowers in the valley,
She saw a sweet babe in the porch,
And the green leaves they grow rarely.

O sweet babe and you were mine,
Fine flowers in the valley,
I would clothe you in the silk so fine
And the green leaves they grow rarely.

O mother dear, when I was yours,
Fine flowers in the valley,
You did not prove to me so kind,
And the green leaves they grow rarely.

The Birches
of Aberfeldie

Now summer shines on flowery hill sides,
And over the crystal streamlets plays,
Come, let us spend the lightsome days
In the birches of Aberfeldie!

Chorus
Lovely girl, will you go,
Will you go, will you go?
Lovely girl, will you go,
To the birches of Aberfeldie?

The little birdies blithely sing,
While over their heads the hazels hang,
Or lightly flit on wanton wing
In the birches of Aberfeldie!

The hill sides ascend like lofty walls,
The foaming stream, deep-roaring, falls
Over hung with fragrant-spreading woods,
The birches of Aberfeldie.

The hoary cliffs are crowned with flowers,
White over the falls the streamlet pours,
And, rising, wets with misty showers
The birches of Aberfeldie.

Let Fortune's gifts at random flee,
They never shall draw a wish from me,
Supremely blest with love and you
In the birches of Aberfeldie.

To a Mountain Daisy

On turning one down with the plough.
In April 1786.

Small, modest, crimson-tipped flower,
You have met me in an evil hour;
For I must crush among the dust
Your slender stem:
To spare you now is past my power,
You lovely gem.

Alas it is not your neighbour sweet,
The bonny lark, companion meet,
Bending you among the dewy wet,
With speckled breast!
When upward springing, blithe, to greet
The purpling east.

Cold blew the bitter-biting north
Upon your early, humble birth;
Yet cheerfully you sparkled forth
Amid the storm,
Scarce reared above the parent-earth
Your tender form.

The flaunting flowers our gardens yield,
High sheltering woods and walls must shield;
But you, beneath the random shelter
Of clod or stone,
Adorns the bare stubble field,
Unseen, alone.

There, in your scanty mantle clad,
Your snowy bosom sun-ward spread,
You lift your unassuming head
　　In humble guise;
But now the plough-share tears up your bed,
　　And low you lie!

Such is the fate of artless maid,
Sweet floweret of the rural shade!
By loves simplicity betrayed,
　　And guileless trust;
Until she, like you, all soiled, is laid
　　Low in the dust.

Such is the fate of simple Bard,
On Life's rough ocean luckless starred!
Unskilled he to note the card
　　Of prudent lore,
Till billows rage, and gales blow hard,
　　And whelm him over.

Such fate to suffering Worth is given,
Who long with wants and woes has striven,
By human pride or cunning driven
　　To miseries brink;
Till, wretched of every stay but Heaven,
　　He, ruined, sink!

Even you who mourns the Daisy's fate,
That fate is yours – no distant date;
Stern Ruin's plough-share drives elate,
　　Full on your bloom,
Till crushed beneath the furrow's weight
　　Shall be your doom!

John Barleycorn

A Ballad

There was three kings into the east,
Three kings both great and high,
And they have sworn a solemn oath
John Barleycorn should die.

They took a plough and ploughed him down,
Put clods upon his head,
And they have sworn a solemn oath
John Barleycorn was dead.

But the cheerful Spring came kindly on,
And showers began to fall;
John Barleycorn got up again,
And sore surprised them all.

The sultry suns of Summer came,
And he grew thick and strong:
His head well armed with pointed spears,
That no one should him wrong.

The sober Autumn entered mild,
When he grew wan and pale;
His bending joints and drooping head
Showed he began to fail.

His colour sickened more and more,
He faded into age;
And then his enemies began
To show their deadly rage.

They have taken a weapon long and sharp,
And cut him by the knee;
Then tied him fast upon a cart,
Like a rogue for forgery.

They laid him down upon his back,
And cudgelled him full sore.
They hung him up before the storm,
And turned him over and over.

They filled up a darksome pit
With water to the brim,
They heaved in John Barleycorn –
There, let him sink or swim!

They laid him out upon the floor,
To work him further woe;
And still, as signs of life appeared,
They toss'd him to and fro.

They wasted over a scorching flame
The marrow of his bones;
But a miller used him worst of all,
For he crushed him between two stones.

...

And they have taken his very heart's blood,
And drank it round and round;
And still the more and more they drank,
Their joy did more abound.

John Barleycorn was a hero bold,
Of noble enterprise;
For if you do but taste his blood,
It will make your courage rise.

It will make a man forget his woes;
It will heighten all his joy:
It will make the widow's heart to sing,
Though the tear were in her eye.

Then let us toast John Barleycorn,
Each man a glass in hand;
And may his great posterity
Ne'er fail in old Scotland!

To a Violet

Go, little flower: go bid your name impart
Each hope, each wish, each beating of my heart;
Go, soothe her sorrows, bid all anguish cease,
Go, be the bearer of yourself – heart's ease.

The Hillside Slopes
of Ballochmyle

The Catrine woods were yellow seen,
The flowers decayed on Catrine lea
No lark sang on hillock green,
But nature sickened on the eye;
Through faded groves Maria sang,
Herself in beauty's bloom the while,
And always the wild-wood echoes rang:–
'Farewell the hillside slopes of Ballochmyle!

'Low in your wintry beds, you flowers,
Again you will flourish fresh and fair;
You birds, dumb in withering bowers,
Again you will charm the vocal air;
But here, alas! for me no more
Shall bird charm, or flowery smile:
Farewell the lovely banks of river Ayr!
Farewell! Farewell sweet Ballochmyle!'

Corn Ridges
Are Lovely

It was upon a Lammas night,
When corn ridges are lovely,
Beneath the moon's unclouded light,
I held away to Annie;
The time flew by, with careless heed;
Till, between the dark and dawn,
With small persuasion she agreed
To see me through the barley.

Chorus
Corn ridges, and barley ridges,
And corn ridges are lovely:
I will never forget that happy night,
Among the ridges with Annie.

The sky was blue, the wind was still,
The moon was shining clearly;
I set her down, with right good will,
Among the ridges of barley:
I knew her heart was all my own;
I loved her most sincerely;
I kissed her over and over again,
Among the ridges of barley.

I locked her in my fond embrace;
　　Her heart was beating rarely:
My blessings on that happy place,
　　Among the ridges of barley.
But by the moon and stars so bright,
　　That shone that hour so clearly!
She ay shall bless that happy night
　　Among the ridges of barley.

I have been blithe with comrades dear;
　　I have been merry drinking;
I have been joyful gathering money;
　　I have been happy thinking:
But all the pleasures ever I saw,
　　Though three times doubled fairly –
That happy night was worth them all,
　　Among the ridges of barley.

Love's Idyll,
Love's Sorrow

A Red, Red Rose

O, my love is like a red, red rose,
That is newly sprung in June.
O, my love is like the melody,
That is sweetly played in tune.

As fair are you, my lovely lass,
So deep in love am I,
And I will love you still, my Dear,
Till all the seas go dry.

Till all the seas go dry, my Dear,
And the rocks melt with the sun!
O I will love you still, my Dear,
While the sands of life shall run.

And fare you well, my only Love,
And fare you well a while!
And I will come again, my Love,
Although it were ten thousand mile!

The Girl
of Ballochmyle

It was evening: the dewy fields were green,
  On every blade the pearls hang,
The zephyr wantoned round the bean,
  And bore its fragrant sweets along,
    In every glen the mavis sang,
All Nature listening seemed the while,
  Except where green-wood echoes rang
Among the hill sides of Ballochmyle.

With careless step I onward strayed,
  My heart rejoiced in Nature's joy,
When musing in a lonely glade,
  A maiden fair I chanced to spy.
Her look was like the Morning's eye,
  Her air like Nature's vernal smile.
Perfection whispered, passing by:–
  'Behold the lass of Ballochmyle!'

Fair is the morning in flowery May,
  And sweet is night in autumn mild,
When roving through the garden gay,
  Or wandering in the lonely wild;
    But women, Nature's darling child –
There all her charms she does compile!
  Even there her other works are foiled
By the lovely lass of Ballochmyle.

O, had she been a country maid,
And I the happy country swain,
Though sheltered in the lowest shed
That ever rose on Scotia's plain,
Through weary winter's wind and rain
With joy, with rapture, I would toil,
And nightly to my bosom strain
The lovely lass of Ballochmyle!

Then pride might climb the slippery steep,
Where fame and honours lofty shine.
And thirst of gold might tempt the deep,
Or downward seek the Indian mine!
Give me the cottage below the pine,
To tend the flocks or till the soil,
And every day have joys divine
With the lovely lass of Ballochmyle.

The Girl
of Cessnock Banks

On Cessnock banks a girl dwells,
Could I describe her shape and mien;
Our girls all she far excels –
And she has two sparkling, roguish eyes!

She is sweeter than the morning dawn,
When rising Phoebus first is seen,
And dew-drops twinkle over the lawn –
And she has two sparkling, roguish eyes!

She is stately like yonder youthful ash,
That grows the cowslip hill-sides between,
And drinks the stream with vigour fresh –
And she has two sparkling, roguish eyes!

She is spotless like the flowering thorn
With flowers so white and leaves so green,
When purest in the dewy morning –
And she has two sparkling, roguish eyes!

Her looks are like the vernal May,
When evening Phoebus shines serene,
While birds rejoice on every spray –
And she has two sparkling, roguish eyes!

Her hair is like the curling mist,
That climbs the mountain-sides at evening,
When flower-reviving rains are past –
And she has two sparkling, roguish eyes!

Her forehead is like the showery bow,
When gleaming sunbeams intervene,
And gild the distant mountain's brow –
And she has two sparkling, roguish eyes!

Her cheeks are like yonder crimson gem,
The pride of all the flowery scene,
Just opening on its thorny stem –
And she has two sparkling, roguish eyes!

Her teeth are like the nightly snow,
When pale the morning rises keen,
While hid the murmuring streamlets flow –
And she has two sparkling, roguish eyes!

Her lips are like yonder cherries ripe,
That sunny walls from Boreas screen:
They tempt the taste and charm the sight –
And she has two sparkling, roguish eyes!

Her breath is like the fragrant breeze,
That gently stirs the blossomed bean,
When Phoebus sinks behind the seas –
And she has two sparkling, roguish eyes!

Her voice is like the evening thrush,
That sings on Cessnock banks unseen,
While his mate sits nestling in the bush –
And she has two sparkling, roguish eyes!

But it is not her air, her form, her face,
Though matching Beauty's fabled Queen:
It is the mind that shines in every grace –
And chiefly in her roguish eyes!

Craigieburn Wood

Sweet closes the evening on Craigieburn Wood
And blithely awakens the morrow;
But the pride of the spring in the Craigieburn Wood
Can yield me nothing but sorrow.

Chorus
Beyond you, dearie, beyond you, dearie,
And O, to be lying beyond you!
O, sweetly, soundly, well may he sleep
That is laid in the bed beyond you!

I see the spreading leaves and flowers,
I hear the wild birds singing;
But pleasure they have none for me,
While care my heart is wringing.

I cannot tell, I must not tell,
I dare not for your anger;
But secret love will break my heart,
If I conceal it longer.

I see you graceful, straight, and tall,
I see you sweet and lovely;
But O, what will my torment be,
If you refuse your Johnie!

To see you in another's arms
In love to lie and languish,
It would be my death, that will be seen –
My heart would burst with anguish!

But, Jeanie, say you will be mine,
Say you loves none before me,
And all my days of life to come
I will gratefully adore you.

For You
Is Laughing Nature

For you is laughing Nature gay,
For you she pours the vernal day:
For me in vain is Nature dressed,
While Joy is a stranger to my breast.

I Do Confess
You Are So Fair

I do confess you are so fair,
I would have been over the ears in love,
Had I not found the slightest prayer
That lips could speak your heart could move.
I do confess you sweet, but find
You are so extravagant of your sweets,
Your favours are the silly wind
That kisses every thing it meets.

See yonder rosebud rich in dew,
Among its native briers so coy,
How soon it loses its scent and hue,
When pulled and worn a common toy!
Such fate ere long shall you betide,
Though you may gaily bloom awhile,
And soon you shall be thrown aside,
Like any common weed, and vile.

Now Rosy May

Now rosy May comes in with flowers
To deck her gay, green-spreading bowers;
And now comes in the happy hours
    To wander with my Davie.

Chorus
Meet me on the Warlock Knoll,
    Dainty Davie, Dainty Davie!
There I will spend the day with you,
    My own dear Dainty Davie.

The crystal waters round us fall,
    The merry birds are lovers all,
The scented breezes round us blow,
    A wandering with my Davie.

When purple morning starts the hare
    To steal upon her early fare,
Then through the dews I will repair
    To meet my faithful Davie.

When day, expiring in the west,
    The curtain draws on Nature's rest,
I flee to his arms I love the best:
    And that is my own dear Davie!

Green Grow
the Rushes, O

Green grow the rushes, O;
Green grow the rushes, O;
The sweetest hours that ever I spend,
Are spent among the girls, O.

There is nothing but care on every hand,
In every hour that passes, O:
What signifies the life of man,
And it were not for the girls, O.

The worldly race may riches chase,
And riches still may fly them, O;
And though at last they catch them fast,
Their hearts can never enjoy them, O.

But give me a quiet hour at evening,
My arms about my dearie, O,
And worldly cares and worldly men
May all go topsy-turvy, O!

For you so grave, you sneer at this;
You are nothing but senseless asses, O;
The wisest man the world ever saw,
He dearly loved the girls, O.

Old Nature swears, the lovely dears
Her noblest work she classes, O:
Her apprentice hand she tried on man,
And then she made the girls, O.

Here Is the Glen

Here is the glen, and here is the bower
　　All underneath the birches shade,
The village-bell has tolled the hour –
　　O, what can stay my lovely maid?
It is not Maria's whispering call –
　　It is but the balmy-breathing gale,
Mixed with some warbler's dying fall
　　The dewy star of evening to hail!

　　It is Maria's voice I hear! –
So calls the woodlark in the grove
　　His little faithful mate to cheer:
At once it is music and it is love!
And are you come? And are you true?
　　O, welcome dear, to love and me,
　　And let us all our vows renew
Along the flowery banks of Cree!

As I Went Out
One May Morning

As I went out one May morning,
A May morning it chanced to be;
There I was aware of a well-favoured maid,
Came dancing over the grass to me.

O, but she was a well-favoured maid,
The loveliest girl that is under the sun;
I asked if she could fancy me,
But her answer was, 'I am too young.'

'To be your bride I am too young,
To be your fellow would shame my relatives,
So therefore pray young man begone,
For you never, never shall my favour win.'

But among yon birches and hawthorns green,
Where roses blow and woodbines hang,
O, there I learned my lovely girl,
That she was not a single hour too young.

The girl blushed, the girl sighed,
And the tear stood twinkling in her eye;
'O kind Sir, since you have done me this wrong,
It is pray when will you marry me.'

'It is of that day take you no heed,
For that is a day you never shall see;
For anything that passed between us two,
You had your share as well as me.'

She wrung her hands, she tore her hair,
She cried out most bitterly,
'O, what will I say to my mother
When I go home with a false story.'

'O, as you malt, so must you brew,
And as you brew, so must you cask:
But come to my arms, my one lovely girl,
For you never shall rue what you now have done.'

Blithe Have I Been on Yonder Hill

Blithe have I been on yonder hill
As the lambs before me,
Careless every thought, and free
As the breeze flew over me.
Now no longer sport and play
Mirth or song can please me:
Lesley is so fair and coy,
Care and anguish seize me.

Heavy, heavy is the task,
Hopeless love declaring!
Trembling, I can do nothing but stare,
Sighing, dumb despairing!
If she will not ease the throes
In my bosom swelling,
Underneath the grass-green sod
Soon must be my dwelling.

O, Were I on Parnassus Hill

O, were I on Parnassus hill,
Or had of Helicon my fill,
That I might catch poetic skill
To sing how dear I love you!
But Nith must be my Muses' well,
My Muse must be my handsome self,
On Corsencon I will gaze and spell,
And write how dear I love you.

Then come, sweet Muse, inspire my lay!
For all the live-long summer's day
I could not sing, I could not say
How much, how dear I love you.
I see you dancing over the green,
Your waist so neat, your limbs so clean,
Your tempting lips, your roguish eyes –
By Heaven and Earth I love you!

By night, by day, a-field, at home,
The thoughts of you my breast inflame,
And always I muse and sing your name –
I only live to love you.
Though I were doomed to wander on,
Beyond the sea, beyond the sun,
Till my last weary sand was run,
Till then – and then – I would love you!

O, Were My Love

O, were my love yon lilac fair
With purple blossoms to the spring,
And I a bird to shelter there,
When wearied on my little wing,
How I would mourn when it was torn
By Autumn wild and Winter rude!
But I would sing on wanton wing,
When youthful May its bloom renewed.

O, if my love were yonder red rose,
That grows upon the castle wall,
And I myself a drop of dew
Into her lovely breast to fall,
O, there, beyond expression blessed,
I would feast on beauty all the night,
Sealed on her silk-soft folds to rest,
Till scared away by Phoebus' light!

Of All the Directions the Wind Can Blow

Of all the directions the wind can blow
I dearly like the west,
For there the lovely girl lives,
The girl I love best.
There wild woods grow, and rivers roll,
And many a hill between,
But day and night my fancy's flight
Is ever with my Jean.

I see her in the dewy flowers –
I see her sweet and fair.
I hear her in the tuneful birds –
I hear her charm the air.
There is not a lovely flower that springs
By fountain, wood, or green,
There is not a lovely bird that sings,
But reminds me of my Jean.

You Lingering Star

You lingering star with lessening ray,
That loves to greet the early morn,
Again you ushers in the day
My Mary from my soul was torn.
O Mary, dear departed shade!
Where is your place of blissful rest?
See you your lover lowly laid?
Hear you the groans that rend his breast?

That sacred hour can I forget,
Can I forget the hallowed grove,
Where by the winding Ayr, we met
To live one day of parting love?
Eternity cannot efface
Those records dear of transports past,
Your image at our last embrace –
Ah! little thought we it was our last!

Ayr, gurgling, kissed his pebbled shore,
Overhung with wild woods thickening green;
The fragrant birch and hawthorn greyish-white
Entwined amorous round the enraptured scene;
The flowers sprang wanton to be pressed,
The birds sang love on every spray,
Till too, too soon, the glowing west
Proclaimed the speed of winged day.

Still over these scenes my memory wakes,
And fondly broods with miser-care.
Time but the impression stronger makes,
As streams their channels deeper wear.
O Mary, dear departed shade!
Where is your place of blissful rest?
See you your lover lowly laid?
Hear you the groans that rend his breast?

On a Bank
of Flowers

On a bank of Flowers in a summer day,
For summer lightly dressed,
The youthful blooming Nelly lay
With love and sleep oppressed;
When Willie, wandering through the wood,
Who for her favour often had sued –
He gazed, he wished,
He feared, he blushed,
And trembled where he stood.

Her closed eyes, like weapons sheathed,
Were sealed in soft repose;
Her lips, still as she fragrant breathed,
It richer dyed the rose;
The springing lilies, sweetly pressed,
Wild-wanton kissed her rival breast:
He gazed, he wished,
He feared, he blushed,
His bosom ill at rest.

Her robes, light-waving in the breeze,
   Her tender limbs embrace;
Her lovely form, her native ease,
   All harmony and grace.
Tumultuous tides his pulses roll,
A faltering, ardent kiss he stole:
      He gazed, he wished,
      He feared, he blushed,
   And sighed his very soul.

As flies the partridge from the brake
   On fear-inspired wings,
So Nelly starting, half-awake,
   Away affrighted springs.
But Willie followed – as he should;
He overtook her in the wood;
      He vowed, he prayed,
      He found the maid
   Forgiving all, and good.

Had I a Cave

Had I a cave
On some wild distant shore,
Where the winds howl
To the wave's dashing roar,
There would I weep my woes,
There seek my lost repose,
Till grief my eyes should close,
Never to wake more!

Falsest of womankind,
Can you declare
All your fond, plighted vows
Fleeting as air?
To your new lover hasten,
Laugh over your perjury,
Then in your bosom try
What peace is there!

My Fiddle and I

Green sleeves and tartan ties
Mark my true love where she lies:
I will be at her or she rise,
My fiddle and I together.

Be it by the crystal stream,
Be it by the milk-white thorn;
I shall wake her in the morning,
My fiddle and I together.

Always Awake, O

Summer is a pleasant time:
Flowers of every colour,
The water runs over the hollow,
And I long for my true lover.

Chorus
Always awake, O,
Awake still and weary:
Sleep I can get nane
For thinking on my dear.

When I sleep I dream,
When I wake I am apprehensive,
Sleep I can get none
For thinking on my dear.

Lonely night comes on,
All the rest are sleeping,
I think on my handsome lad,
And I blur my eyes with weeping.

The Chevalier's Lament
/ The Small Birds

The small birds rejoice in the green leaves returning,
The murmuring streamlet winds clear through the vale,
The primroses blow in the dews of the morning,
But wild scattered cowslips bedeck the green dale:
But what can give pleasure, or what can seem fair,
When the lingering moments are numbered by care?
No flowers gaily springing,
Nor birds sweetly singing
Can soothe the sad bosom of joyless despair!

The deed that I dared, could it merit their malice,
A king and a father to place on his throne?
His right are these hills, and his right are those valleys,
Where the wild beasts find shelter, though I can find none!
But it is not my sufferings thus wretched, forlorn –
My brave gallant friends, it is your ruin I mourn!
Your faith proved so loyal
In hot bloody trial,
Alas! can I make it no better return?

The Winter
It Is Past

The winter it is past, and the summer comes at last,
    And the small birds sing on every tree:
The hearts of these are glad, but mine is very sad,
    For my love is parted from me.

The rose upon the brier by the waters running clear
    May have charms for the linnet or the bee:
Their little loves are blessed, and their little hearts at rest,
    But my lover is parted from me

My love in like the sun in the firmament does run –
    Forever is constant and true;
But his is like the moon, that wanders up and down,
    And every month it is new.

All you that are in love, and cannot it remove,
    I pity the pains you endure,
For experience makes me know that your hearts are full of woe,
    A woe that no mortal can cure.

Sweet Falls the Evening

Sweet falls the evening on Craigieburn,
And blithe awakes the morrow,
But all the pride of Spring's return
Can yield me nothing but sorrow.

I see the flowers and spreading trees,
I hear the wild birds singing;
But what a weary person can please,
And Care his bosom is wringing?

Fondly, fondly would I my grief's impart,
Yet dare not for your anger;
But secret love will break my heart,
If I conceal it longer.

If you refuse to pity me,
If you should love another,
When yonder green leaves fade from the tree,
Around my grave they will wither.

A Wakeful Mother

'Where are you going, my lovely lass?
Where are you going, my honey?'
She answered me right saucily: -
An errand for my mother!'

'O, where live you, my lovely lass?
O, where live you, my honey?'
'By yon stream side, if you must know,
In a little house with my mother!'

But I went up the glen at evening
To see my lovely lassie,
And long before the grey morning came
She was not half so saucy.

O, woe befall the wakeful cock,
And the polecat stop his crowing!
He awakened the old woman from her sleep
A little bit before the dawning.

An angry wife I know she raised,
And over the bed she brought her,
And with a big hazel cudgel
She made her a well thrashed daughter.

'O, fare-you-well, my lovely lass!
O, fare-you-well, my honey!
You are a gay and a lovely lass,
But you have a wakeful mother!'

The Seasons

Bonny Bell

The smiling Spring comes in rejoicing,
    And surly Winter grimly flies;
Now crystal clear are the falling waters,
    And bonny blue are the sunny skies.
Fresh o'er the mountains breaks forth the morning,
    The ev'ning gilds the ocean's swell;
All creatures joy in the sun's returning,
    And I rejoice in my bonny Bell.

The flowery Spring leads sunny Summer,
    The yellow Autumn presses near;
Then in his turn comes gloomy Winter,
    Till smiling Spring again appear:
Thus seasons dancing, life advancing,
    Old Time and Nature their changes tell;
But never ranging, still unchanging,
    I adore my bonny Bell.

Now Spring
Has Clad

Now spring has clad the grove in green,
And strewed the meadow with flowers;
The furrowed, waving corn is seen
Rejoice in fostering showers;
While everything in nature join
Their sorrows to forego,
O, why thus all alone are mine
The weary steps of woe!

The trout within yonder meandering steam
Glides swift, a silver dart,
And, safe beneath the shady thorn,
Defies the anglers art:
My life was once that careless stream,
That wanton trout was I,
But Love with unrelenting beam
Has scorched my fountains dry.

The little floweret's peaceful lot,
In yonder cliff that grows,
Which save the linnet's flight, I know,
No ruder visit knows,
Was mine, till Love has over me past,
And blighted all my bloom;
And now beneath the withering blast
My youth and joy consume.

The wakened lark warbling springs,
And climbs the early sky,
Winnowing blithe his dewy wings
In Morning's rosy eye:
As little heeded I Sorrow's power,
Until the flowery snare
Of witching Love in luckless hour
Made me the slave of care!

O, had my fate been Greenland snows
Or Africa's burning zone,
With Man and Nature leagued my foes,
So Peggy never I had known!
The wretch, whose doom is 'hope no more',
What tongue his woes can tell,
Within whose bosom, save Despair,
No kinder spirits dwell!

It Was the
Charming Month of May

It was the charming month of May,
When all the flowers were fresh and gay,
One morning, by the break of day,
The youthful, charming Chloe,
From peaceful slumber she arose,
Girt on her mantle and her hose,
And over the flowery meadow she goes –
The youthful, charming Chloe!

Chorus
Lovely was she by the dawn,
Youthful Chloe, charming Chloe,
Tripping over the pearly lawn,
The youthful charming Chloe.

The feathered people you might see
Perched all around on every tree!
With notes of sweetest melody
They hail the charming Chloe,
Till, painting gay the eastern skies,
The glorious sun began to rise,
Out-rivalled by the radiant eyes
Of youthful, charming Chloe.

In Summer,
When the Hay Was Mown

In summer, when the hay was mown
And corn waved green in every field,
While clover blooms white over the pasture,
And roses blow in every sheltered spot,
Blithe Bessie in the milking shed
Says:– 'I will be wed, come of it what will!'
Out spoke a dame in wrinkled old age:–
'Of good advisement comes no ill.'

'It is you have wooers many a one,
And girl, you are but young, you know!
Then wait a little, and sensibly choose
A well-stocked kitchen, a well-stocked parlour.
There is Johnie of the Buskie-Glen,
Full is his barn, full is his byre,
Take this from me, my lovely hen:
It is plenty that beats the lover's fire!'

'For Johnie of the Buskie-Glen
I do not care a single fly:
He loves so well his crops and cattle,
He has no love to spare for me.
But blithe the glance of Robie's eye,
And well I know he loves me dear:
One glance of him I would not give
For Buskie-Glen and all his gear.'

...

'O thoughtless girl, life is a fight!
The quietest way, the strife is sore.
But always full handed is fighting best:
A hungry care is a terrible care.
But some will spend, and some will spare,
And willful folk must have their will.
Then as you brew, my maiden fair,
Keep mind that you must drink the ale!'

'O, wealth will buy me ridges of land,
And wealth will buy me sheep and cattle!
But the tender heart of pleasant love
The gold and silver can not buy!
We may be poor, Robie and I;
Light is the burden love lays on;
Content and loove brings peace and joy;
What more have Queens upon a throne?'

Song:
Composed in August

Now western winds and slaughtering guns
    Bring Autumn's pleasant weather;
The moorcock springs on whirring wings
    Among the blooming heather:
Now waving grain, wide over the plain,
    Delights the weary farmer;
The moon shines bright, as I roam by night
    To muse upon my charmer.

The partridge loves the fruitful fells,
    The plover loves the mountains;
The woodcock haunts the lonely dells,
    The soaring heron the fountains;
Through lofty groves the wild pigeon roves,
    The path of man to shun it;
The hazel bush overhangs the thrush,
    The spreading thorn the linnet.

Thus every kind their pleasure find,
    The savage and the tender;
Some social join, and leagues combine,
    Some solitary wander:
Move on, away, the cruel sway!
    Tyrannical man's dominion!
The sportsman's joy, the murdering cry,
    The fluttering, gory pinion!

...

But, Peggy dear, the evening is clear,
   Thick flies the skimming swallow,
   The sky is blue, the fields in view
     All fading-green and yellow:
   Come let us stray our glad way,
     And view the charms of Nature;
   The rustling corn, the fruited thorn,
     And every happy creature.

We will gently walk, and sweetly talk,
   While the silent moon shines clearly;
I will clasp your waist, and, fondly pressed,
     Swear how I love you dearly:
Not vernal showers to budding flowers,
     Not Autumn to the farmer,
   So dear can be as you to me,
     My fair, my lovely charmer!

Address to
the Shade of Thomson

On crowning his bust with a wreath of bays,
at Ednam, Roxburghshire.

While virgin Spring by Eden's flood
Unfolds her tender mantle green,
Or dresses the sod in frolic mood,
Or tunes Eolian strains between:

While Summer, with a matron grace,
Retreats to Dryburgh's cooling shade,
Yet often, delighted, stops to trace
The progress of the spikey blade:

While Autumn, benefactor kind,
By Tweed erects his aged head,
And sees, with self-approving mind,
Each creature on his bounty fed:

While maniac Winter rages over
The hills whence classic Yarrow flows,
Rousing the turbid torrent's roar,
Or sweeping, wild, a waste of snows:

So long, sweet Poet of the year!
Shall bloom that wreath you well has won;
While Scotia, with exulting tear,
Proclaims that Thomson was her son.

From:
The Brigs of Ayr

It was when the stacks get on their winter wrap,
And thatch and rope secure the toil-won crop;
Potato heaps are snugged up from damage
Of coming winter's biting, frosty breath;
The bees rejoicing over their summer toils –
Unnumbered buds' an flowers' delicious spoils,
Sealed up with frugal care in massive waxen piles –
Are doomed by man, that tyrant over the weak,
The death of devils smothered with brimstone smoke:
The thundering guns are heard on every side,
The wounded coveys, reeling, scatter wide;
The feathered field-mates, bound by Nature's tie,
Sires, mothers, children, in one carnage lie:
(What warm, poetic heart but inside bleeds,
And execrates man's savage, ruthless deeds!)
No more the flower in field or meadow springs;
No more the grove with airy concert rings,
Except perhaps the robin's whistling glee,
Proud of the height of some small half-grown tree;
The hoary mornings proceed the sunny days;
Mild, calm, serene, wide-spreads the noontide blaze,
While thick the gossamer waves wanton in the rays.

The Lazy Mist

The lazy mist hangs from the brow of the hill,
Concealing the course of the dark winding rill.
How languid the scenes, late so sprightly, appear,
As Autumn to Winter resigns the pale year!

The forests are leafless, the meadows are brown,
And all the gay foppery of summer is flown.
Apart let me wander, apart let me muse,
How quick Time is flying, how keen Fate pursues!

How long I have lived, but how much lived in vain!
How little of life's scanty span may remain!
What aspects old Time in his progress has worn!
What ties cruel Fate in my bosom has torn!

How foolish, or worse, till our summit is gained!
And downward, how weakened, how darkened, how pained!
Life is not worth having with all it can give:
For something beyond it poor man, sure, must live.

From:
Tam O'Shanter

Burns's famous narrative poem is most likely set on
a Halloween, when in Scottish folklore witches met and
danced with the Devil. Here Tam sets off from the inn,
somewhat worse for wear.

But pleasures are like poppies spread:
You seize the flower, it's bloom is shed;
Or like the snow falls in the river,
A moment white – then melts for ever;
Or like the Borealis, race,
That flit before you can point their place;
Or like the rainbow's lovely form
Vanishing amid the storm.
No man can tether time or tide;
The hour approaches Tam must ride:
That hour, of night's black arch the key-stone
That dreary hour Tam mounts his beast in;
And such a night he takes the road in,
As never poor sinner was abroad in.

The wind blew as it would have blown its last;
The rattling showers rose on the blast;
The speedy gleams the darkness swallowed;
Loud, deep, and long the thunder bellowed:
That night, a child might understand,
The Devil had business on his hand.

Cold Is the Evening Blast

Cold is the evening blast
Of Boreas over the pool,
And dawning it is dreary,
When birches are bare at Christmas time.

O, cold blows the evening blast,
When bitter bites the frost,
And in the dark and dreary drift
The hills and glens are lost!

Never so darkly blew the night
That drifted over the hill,
But lovely Peg of Ramsay
Got grist to her mill.

From:
Address to the Deil

When thaws dissolve the snowy hoard.
And float the jingling icy surface,
Then, water fairies haunt the ford,
By your direction,
And travellers in the night are lured
To their destruction.

And often your bog traversing jack-o'-lanterns
Decoy the person that late and drunk is:
The blazing, cursed, mischievous monkeys
Delude his eyes,
Until in some miry bog he sunk is,
Never more to rise.

From: Tam O'Shanter

Tam witnesses a 'witching hour' meeting
of the local coven in a kirk (church).

Wizards and witches in a dance:
No cotillion, brand new from France,
But hornpipes, jigs, strathspeys, and reels,
Put life and mettle in their heels.
A window seat in the east,
There sat the Old Devil, in shape of beast;
A shaggy dog, black, grim, and large,
To give them music was his charge:
He screwed the bagpipes and made them squeal,
Till roof and rafters all did ring.
Coffins stood around, like open cupboards,
That showed the dead in their last dresses;
And, by some devilish magic device,
Each in its cold hand held a light:
By which heroic Tam was able
To note upon the holy table,
A murderer's bones, in gallows-irons;
Two span-long, little, unchristened children;
A thief new-cut from a gallows rope –
With his last gasp his mouth did gape;
Five tomahawks with blood red-rusted;
Five scimitars with murder crusted;
A garter which a babe had strangled;
A knife a father's throat had mangled –
Whom his own son of life bereft –
The grey hairs still stuck to the heft;
With more of horrible and awful,
Which even to name would be unlawful.

Three lawyers' tongues, turned inside out,
  With lies seamed like a beggar's cloth;
Three Priests' hearts, rotten, black as muck,
  Lay stinking, vile, in every corner.

Up in the
Morning Early

Cold blows the wind from east to west,
  The drift is driving sorely,
So loud and shrill is I hear the blast –
  I am sure it is winter fairly!

Chorus
Up in the morning's not for me,
  Up in the morning early!
When all the hills are covered with snow.
  I am sure it is winter fairly!

The birds sit shivering in the thorn,
  All day they fare but sparely;
And long is the night from evening to morning –
  I am sure it is winter fairly!

The Winter of Life

But lately seen in beautiful green,
The woods rejoiced the day;
Through gentle showers the laughing flowers
In double pride were gay;
But now our joys are fled
On winter blasts away,
Yet maiden May in rich array
Again shall bring them all.

But my white head – no kindly thaw
Shall melt the snows of Age!
My trunk of old age, without bush and shelter,
Sinks in Time's wintry rage.
O, Age has weary days
And nights of sleepless pain!
You golden time of youthful prime,
Why comes you not again?

Winter:
a Dirge

The wintry west extends his blast,
And hail and rain does blow;
Or the stormy north sends driving forth
The blinding sleet and snow:
Wild-tumbling brown, the stream comes down,
And roars from bank to slope:
While bird and beast in covert rest,
And pass the heartless day.

'The sweeping blast, the sky overcast,'
The joyless winter day
Let others fear, to me more dear
Than all the pride of May:
The tempest's howl, it soothes my soul,
My griefs it seems to join;
The leafless trees my fancy please,
Their fate resembles mine!

You Power Supreme, whose mighty scheme
These woes of mine fulfil,
Here, firm I rest, they must be best,
Because they are Thy will!
Then all I want (O, do Thou grant
This one request of mine!):
Since to enjoy You do deny,
Assist me to resign.

Farmers
and Cottars

The Gardener
with His Spade

When rosy May comes in with flowers
To deck her gay, green-spreading bowers,
Then busy, busy are his hours,
The gardener with his spade.

The crystal waters gently fall,
The merry birds are lovers all,
The scented breezes round him blow –
The gardener with his spade.

When purple morning starts the hare
To steal upon her early fare,
Then through the dew he must repair –
The gardener with his spade.

When Day, expiring in the west,
The curtain draws on Nature's rest.
He flies to her arms he loves best,
The gardener with his spade.

A Winter Night

When Boreas, cruel and hard,
Sharp shivers through the leafless bower;
When Phoebus gives a short-lived stare,
Far south the horizon,
Dim-darkening through the flaky shower
Or whirling drift:

One night the storm the steeples rocked;
Poor Labour sweet in sleep was locked;
While brooks, with snowy wreaths up-choked,
Wild eddying swirl,
Or, through the mining outlet vomited,
Down headlong hurl:

Listening the doors and windows rattle,
I thought me on the shivering cattle,
Or helpless sheep, who wait this noisy onset
Of winter war,
And through the drift, deep-lairing, scramble
Beneath a jutting rock.

Each hopping bird – little, helpless thing! –
That in the merry months of spring
Delighted me to hear you sing,
What comes of you?
Where will you cower the shivering wing,
And close your eye?

Even you, on murdering errands toiled,
Alone from your savage homes exiled,
The blood-stained roost and sheep pen spoiled
        My heart forgets,
    While pitiless the tempest wild
        Sore on you beats!

Now Phoebe, in her midnight reign,
Dark-muffled, viewed the dreary plain;
Still crowding thoughts, a pensive train.
        Rose in my soul,
    When on my ear this plaintive strain,
        Slow-solemn, stole:

'Blow, blow, you winds, with heavier gust!
And freeze, you bitter biting frost!
Descend, you chilly, smothering snows!
Not all your rage, as now united, shows
    More hard unkindness unrelenting,
    Vengeful malice, unrepenting,
Than heaven-illumined Man on brother Man bestows!
        ...

See stern Oppression's iron grip,
Or mad Ambition's gory hand,
Sending, like blood-hounds from the slip,
Woe, Want, and Murder over a land!
Even in the peaceful rural vale,
Truth, weeping, tells the mournful tale:
How pampered Luxury, Flattery by her side,
The parasite poisoning her ear,
With all the servile wretches in the rear,
Looks over proud Property, extended wide;
And eyes the simple, rustic ploughman,
Whose toil upholds the glittering show –
A creature of another kind,
Some coarser substance, unrefined –
Placed for her lordly use, thus far, thus vile, below!

Where, where is Love's fond, tender throe,
With lordly Honor's lofty brow,
The powers you proudly own?
Is there, beneath Love's noble name,
Can harbour, dark, the selfish aim,
To bless himself alone?
Mark Maiden-Innocence a prey
To love-pretending snares:
This boasted Honor turns away,
Shunning soft Pity's rising sway,
Regardless of the tears and unavailing prayers!
Perhaps this hour, in Misery's squalid nest,
She strains your infant to her joyless breast,
And with a mother's fears shrinks at the rocking blast!

'O you! who, sunk in beds of down,
Feel not a want but what yourselves create,
Think, for a moment, on his wretched fate,
Whom friends and fortune quite disown!
Ill-satisfied keen nature's clamorous call,
Stretched on his straw, he lays himself to sleep;
While through the ragged roof and cracked wall,
Chill, over his slumbers piles the drifting heap!
Think on the dungeon's grim confine,
Where Guilt and poor Misfortune pine!
Guilt, erring man, relenting view!
But shall your legal rage pursue
The wretch, already crushed low
By cruel Fortune's undeserved blow?
Affliction's sons are brothers in distress;
A brother to relieve, how exquisite the bliss!'

I heard no more, for Chanticleer
Shook off the powdery snow,
And hailed the morning with a cheer,
A cottage-rousing crow.
But deep this truth impressed my mind:
Through all His works abroad,
The heart benevolent and kind
The most resembles God.

A Ruined Farmer

The sun he is sunk in the west,
All creatures retired to rest,
While here I sit, all sore beset
With sorrow, grief, and woe:
And it is O fickle Fortune, O!

The prosperous man is asleep,
Nor hears how the whirlwinds sweep;
But Misery and I must watch
The surly tempests blow:
And it is O fickle Fortune, O!

There lies the dear Partner of my breast,
Her cares for a moment at rest!
Must I see you, my youthful pride,
Thus brought so very low? –
And it is O fickle Fortune, O!

There lie my sweet babies in her arms:
No anxious fear their little hearts alarms;
But for their sake my heart does ache,
With many a bitter throe:
And it is O fickle Fortune, O!

I once was by Fortune cared,
I once could relieve the distressed;
Now life's poor support, hardly earned,
My fate will scarce bestow:
And it is O fickle Fortune, O!

No comfort, no comfort I have!
How welcome to me were the grave!
But then my wife and children dear –
O, whither would they go?
And it is O fickle Fortune, O!

O, whither, O, whither shall I turn,
All friendless, forsaken, forlorn?
For in this world Rest of Peace
I never more shall know:
And it is O fickle Fortune, O!

At Friars
Carse Hermitage

To Riddell, much-lamented man,
This ivied cot was dear:
Wanderer, do you value matchless worth?
This ivied cot revere.

Robin Reaped
in the Harvest

I went up to Dunse
To warp a web of coarse woollen,
At his daddy's gate
Who met me but Robin!

Chorus
Robin reaped in the harvest,
I reaped with him:
Not a sickle had I,
Yet I stuck by him.

Was not Robin bold,
Though I was a cottager?
Played me such a trick,
And me the Elder's daughter!

Robin promised me
All my winter food:
Not a thing he had but three
Goose quills and a knife!

O, Can
You Labour Land

I hired a man at Martinmas
With hansel-pennies three;
But all the fault I had to him
He could not labour land.

Chorus
O, can you labour land, young man,
O, can you labour land?
Go back the way you came again –
You shall never scorn me!

O, stroking is good in February,
And kissing is sweet in May;
But what signifies a young man's love,
If it does not last for always?

O, kissing is the key of love
And stroking is the lock;
And making of it is the best thing
That ever a young thing got!

From:
The Vision

The sun had closed the winter day,
The curlers ceased their roaring play,
And hungered hare taken her way,
To kitchen gardens green,
While faithless snows each step betray
Where she has been.

The thresher's weary flail,
The live long day had tired me;
And when the day had closed his eye,
Far in the west,
Back in the parlour, right pensively,
I went to rest.

There, lonely by the fire side,
I sat and eyed the spewing smoke,
That filled, with cough provoking smoke,
The old clay structure;
And heard the restless rats squeak
About the rooftree.

All in this dusty, misty climate,
I backward mused on wasted time:
How I had spent my youthful prime,
And done nothing,
But stringing nonsense up in rhyme,
For fools to sing.

From:
The Cotter's Saturday Night

November chill blows loud with angry wail;
  The shortening winter-day is near a close;
The miry beasts retreating from the plough;
The blackening trains of crows to their repose:
The toil-worn Cotter from his labour goes –
  This night his weekly toil is at an end,
Collects his spades, his pickaxes, and his hoes,
  Hoping the morn in ease and rest to spend,
And weary, over the moor, his course does
        homeward bend.

Old Rob Morris

There is Old Rob Morris that dwells in yonder glen,
He is the king of good fellows and pick of old men:
He has gold in his coffers, he has oxen and cattle,
And one lovely girl, his pet and mine.

She is as fresh as the morning the fairest in May,
She is sweet as the evening among the new hay,
And blithe and as artless as the lambs on the meadow,
And dear to my heart as the light to my eye.

But O, she is an heiress, old Robin is a laird
And my daddy has nothing but a cottage-house and garden!
A wooer like me must not hope to come fast:
The wounds I must hide that will soon be my death.

The day comes to me, but delight brings me none;
The night comes to me, but my rest it is gone;
I wander my alone like a night-troubled ghost,
And I sigh as my heart it would burst in my breast.

O, had she but been of a lower degree,
I then might have hoped she would have smiled upon me!
O, how past describing had then been my bliss,
As now my distraction no word can express!

What Will I Do
Gin My Hoggie Die

What will I do gin my Hoggie die,
My joy, my pride, my Hoggie:
My only beast, I had nae mae,
And vow but I was vogie.

The lee-lang night we watch'd the fauld,
Me and my faithfu' doggie;
We heard nought but the roaring linn
Amang the braes sae scroggie.

But the houlet cry'd frae the Castle-wa',
The blitter frae the boggie,
The tod reply'd upon the hill,
I trembled for my Hoggie.

When day did daw and cocks did craw,
The morning it was foggie;
An unco tyke lap o'er the dyke
And maist has kill'd my Hoggie.

Rivers
and Streams

Sweet Afton

Flow gently, sweet Afton, among your green slopes!
Flow gently, I will sing you a song in your praise!
My Mary is asleep by the murmuring stream –
Flow gently, sweet Afton, disturb not her dream!

You stock dove whose echo resounds through the glen,
You wild whistling blackbirds in yonder thorny den
You green crested lapwing, your screaming forbear –
I charge you, disturb not my slumbering fair!

How lofty, sweet Afton, your neighbouring hills,
Far marked with the courses of clear, winding rills!
There daily I wander, as noon rises high,
My flocks and my Mary's sweet cottage in my eye.

How pleasant thy banks and green valleys below,
Where wild in the woodlands the primrose blow:
There often, as mild evening weeps over the lea,
The sweet scented birch trees shades my Mary and me.

Your crystal stream, Afton, how lovely it glides,
And winds by the cottage where my Mary resides!
How sportive your waters her snowy feet wash,
As, gathering sweet flowerets, she stems thy clear wave!

Flow gently, sweet Afton, among your green slopes!
Flow gently, sweet river, the theme of my poem!
My Mary is asleep by your murmuring stream –
Flow gently, sweet Afton, disturb not her dream!

Sweet Are the Banks

Sweet are the banks, the banks of Doon,
The spreading flowers are fair,
And everything is blithe and glad,
But I am full of care.
You will break my heart, you lovely bird,
That sings upon the bough!
You remind me of the happy days
When my false Love was true.
You will break my heart, you lovely bird,
That sings beside your mate,
For so I sat, and so I sang,
And knew not of my fate!

Often have I roved by lovely Doon,
To see the woodbine twine,
And each bird sang of its love,
And so did I of mine.
With lightsome heart I pulled a rose
Upon its thorny tree,
But my false lover stole my rose,
And left the thorn with me.
With lightsome heart I pulled a rose
Upon a morning in June,
And so I flourished on the morning,
And so was pulled before noon.

The Banks of Doon

You banks and sides of bonny Doon,
How can you bloom so fresh and fair?
How can you chant, you little birds,
And I so weary full of care!
You will break my heart, you warbling bird,
That flies through the flowering thorn!
You remind me of departed joys,
Departed never to return.

Often have I roved by bonny Doon
To see the rose and woodbine twine,
And every bird sang of its love,
And fondly so did I of mine.
With lightsome heart I plucked a rose,
Full sweet upon its thorny tree!
And my false lover stole my rose –
But ah! he left the thorn with me.

As Down the Stream

As down the stream they took their way,
And through the flowery dale;
His cheek to hers he often did lay,
And love was always the tale,
With:– 'Mary, when shall we return,
Such pleasure to renew?'
Said Mary:– 'Love, I like the stream,
And always shall follow you.'

You Flowery Banks

You flowery banks for lovely Doon,
How can you bloom so fair?
How can you chant, you little birds,
And I so full of care?

You will break my heart, you lovely bird,
That sings upon the bough:
You remind me of the happy days
When my false Love was true!

You will break my heart, you lovely bird,
That sings beside thy mate:
For so I sat, and so I sang,
And knew not of my fate!

Often have I roved by lovely Doon
To see the woodbine twine,
And each bird sang of its love,
And so did I of mine.

With lightsome heart I pulled a rose
From off its thorny tree,
And my false lover stole my rose,
But left the thorn with me.

The Banks of Nith

The Thames flows proudly to the sea,
    Where royal cities stately stand;
But sweeter flows the Nith to me,
Where Cummins once had high command.
    When shall I see that honoured land,
    That winding stream I love so dear?
    Must wayward Fortune's adverse hand
        For ever – ever keep me here?

How lovely, Nith, thy fruitful vales,
    Where bounding hawthorns gaily bloom,
And sweetly spread your sloping dales,
Where lambs wanton through the broom!
Though wandering now must be my doom
    Far from your lovely banks and slopes,
    May there my latest hours consume
        Among my friends of early days!

The Banks
of the Devon

How pleasant the banks of the clear winding Devon,
With green spreading bushes and flowers blooming fair!
But the bonniest flower on the banks of the Devon
Was once a sweet bud on the slopes of the Ayr.
Mild be the sun on this sweet blushing flower,
In the gay rosy morning, as it bathes in the dew!
And gentle the fall of the soft vernal shower,
That steals on the evening each leaf to renew!

O, spare the dear blossom, you orient breezes,
With chill, hoary wing as you usher the dawn!
And far be you distant, you reptile that seizes
The verdure and pride of the garden or lawn!
Let Bourbon exult in his gay gilded lilies,
And England triumphant display her proud rose!
A fairer than either adorns the green valleys,
Where Devon, sweet Devon, meandering flows.

The Humble Petition of Bruar Water to the Noble Duke of Athole

My lord, I know, your noble ear
    Woe never assails in vain;
Emboldened thus, I beg you will hear
    Your humble slave complain,
How saucy Phoebus' scorching beams,
    In flaming summer-pride,
Dry-withering, waste my foamy streams,
    And drink my crystal tide.

The lightly-jumping, staring trout,
    That through my waters play,
If, in their random, playful spouts,
    They near the margin stray;
If, by unlucky chance! they linger long,
    I am scorching up so shallow,
They are left the whitening stones among
    In grasping death to wallow.

Last day I wept with spite and vexation,
    As Poet Burns came by,
That, to a Bard, I should be seen
    With half my channel dry;
A panegyric rhyme, I think,
    Even as I was, he offered me;
But had I in my glory been,
    He, kneeling, would adored me.

...

Here, foaming down the shelving rocks,
In twisting strength I run;
There high my boiling torrent smokes,
Wild-roaring over a water-fall:
Enjoying large each spring and well,
As Nature gave them to me,
I am, although I say it myself,
Worth going a mile to see.

Would, then, my noble master please
To grant my highest wishes,
He will shade my banks with towering trees
And lovely spreading bushes.
Delighted doubly then, my lord,
You will wander on my banks,
And listen to many a grateful bird
Return you tuneful thanks.

The sober lark, warbling wild,
Shall to the skies aspire;
The goldfinch, Music's gayest child,
Shall sweetly join the choir;
The blackbird strong, the linnet clear,
The mavis mild and mellow,
The robin, pensive Autumn cheer
In all her locks of yellow.

This, too, a covert shall ensure
To shield them from the storm;
And coward hare sleep secure,
Low in her grassy form:
Here shall the shepherd make his seat
To weave his crown of flowers;
Or find a sheltering, safe retreat
From prone-descending showers.

And here, by sweet, endearing stealth,
Shall meet the loving pair,
Despising worlds with all their wealth,
As empty idle care:
The flowers shall vie, in all their charms,
The hour of heaven to grace;
And birches extend their fragrant arms
To screen the dear embrace.

Here by chance too, at vernal dawn,
Some musing Bard may stray,
And eye the smoking, dewy lawn
And misty mountain grey;
Or, by the reaper's nightly beam,
Mild-chequering through the trees,
Rave to my darkly dashing stream,
Hoarse-swelling on the breeze.

Let lofty firs and ashes cool
My lowly banks overspread,
And view, deep-bending in the pool,
Their shadows' watery bed:
Let fragrant birches, in woodbines dressed,
My craggy cliffs adorn,
And, for the little songster's nest,
The close embowering thorn!

So may, old Scotia's darling hope,
Your little angel band
Spring, like their fathers, up to prop
Their honoured native land!
So may, through Albion's farthest range of sight,
To social-flowing glasses,
The grace be: 'Athole's honest men
And Athole's lovely girls!'

Logan Water

O Logan, sweetly did you glide
That day I was my Willie's bride,
And years since then have over us run
Like Logan to the summer sun.
But now your flowery banks appear
Like dull winter, dark and dreary,
While my dear lad must face his foes
Far, far from me and Logan hillsides.

Again the merry month of May
Has made our hills and valleys gay;
The birds rejoice in leafy bowers,
The bees hum round the breathing flowers;
Blithe Morning lifts his rosy eye,
And Evening tears are tears of joy:
My soul with no delight all surveys,
While Willie is far from Logan hillsides.

Within yonder milk-white hawthorn bush,
Among her nestlings sits the thrush:
Her faithful mate will share her toil,
Or with his song her cares beguile.
But I with my sweet nurslings here,
No mate to help, no mate to cheer,
Pass widowed nights and joyless days,
While Willie is far from Logan hillsides.

O, woe upon you, Men of State,
That brethren rouse in deadly hate!
As you make many a fond heart mourn,
So may it on your heads return!
You remember not amid your cruel joys
The widow's tears, the orphan's cries;
But soon may peace bring happy days,
And Willie home to Logan hillsides,

Farewell to the Banks of Ayr

The gloomy night is gath'ring fast,
Loud roars the wild, inconstant blast,
Yon murky cloud is foul with rain,
I see it driving o'er the plain;
The hunter now has left the moor.
The scatt'red coveys meet secure,
While here I wander, pressed with care,
Along the lonely banks of Ayr.

The autumn mourns her rip'ning corn
By early winter's ravage torn;
Across her placid, azure sky,
She sees the scowling tempest fly:
Chill runs my blood to hear it rave,
I think upon the stormy wave,
Where many a danger I must dare,
Far from the bonny banks of Ayr.

'Tis not the surging billow's roar,
'Tis not that fatal, deadly shore;
Tho' death in ev'ry shape appear,
The wretched have no more to fear:
But round my heart the ties are bound,
That heart transpierc'd with many a wound;
These bleed afresh, those ties I tear,
To leave the bonny banks of Ayr.

Farewell, old Coila's hills and dales,
Her healthy moors and winding vales;
The scenes where wretched fancy roves,
Pursuing past, unhappy loves!
Farewell, my friends! farewell, my foes!
My peace with these, my love with those,
The bursting tears my heart declare,
Farewell, the bonny banks of Ayr!

The
Wandering Poet

From:
The Holy Fair

Upon a summer Sunday morning,
When Nature's face is fair,
I walked forth to view the corn,
And sniff the fresh air.
The rising sun, over Galston Moors,
With glorious light was glinting;
The hares were hopping down the furrows,
The larks they were chanting
Full sweet that day.

A Rose-bud,
by My Early Walk

A rose-bud, by my early walk
Down a corn-enclosed field-path,
So gently bent its thorny stalk,
All on a dewy morning.
Ere twice the shades of dawn are fled,
In all its crimson glory spread
And drooping rich the dewy head,
It scents the early morning.

Within the bush her covert nest
A little linnet fondly pressed,
The dew sat chilly on her breast,
So early in the morning.
She soon shall see her tender brood,
The pride, the pleasure of the wood,
Among the fresh green leaves bedewed,
Awake the early morning.

So you, dear bird, young Jeany fair,
On trembling string or vocal air
Shall sweetly pay the tender care
That guards your early morning!
So you, sweet rose-bud, young and gay,
Shall beauteous blaze upon the day,
And bless the parent's evening ray
That watched your early morning!

Down the Winding River Nith

Down winding river Nith I did wander
To mark the sweet flowers as they spring.
Down winding river Nith I did wander
Of Phillis to muse and to sing.

Away with your belles and your beauties –
They never with her can compare!
Whoever have met with my Phillis
Has met with the Queen of the Fair!

The Daisy amused my fond fancy,
So artless, so simple, so wild:
'You emblem,' said I, 'of my Phillis' –
For she is Simplicity's child.

The rose-bud is the blush of my charmer,
Her sweet balmy lip when it is pressed.
How fair and how pure is the lily!
But fairer and purer her breast.

Yonder knot of gay flowers in the arbour,
They never with my Phillis can vie:
Her breath is the breath of the woodbine,
Its dew-drop of diamond her eye.

Her voice is the song of the morning,
That wakes through the green-spreading grove,
When Phebus peeps over the mountains
On music, and pleasure, and love.

But Beauty, how frail and how fleeting!
The bloom of a fine summer's day!
While Worth in the mind of my Phillis
Will flourish without a decay.

Verses Written with a Pencil Over the Chimney-Piece, in the Parlour of the Inn at Kenmore, Taymouth

Admiring Nature in her wildest grace,
These northern scenes with weary feet I trace;
Over many a winding dale and painful steep,
The abodes of coveyed grouse and timid sheep,
My savage journey, curious, I pursue,
Till famed Breadalbane opens to my view.
The meeting cliffs each deep-sunk glen divides:
The woods, wild-scattered, clothe their ample sides;
The outstretching lake, imbosomed among the hills,
The eye with wonder and amazement fills:
The Tay meandering sweet in infant pride,
The palace rising on his verdant side,
The lawns wood-fringed in Nature's native taste,
The hillocks dropped in Nature's careless haste,
The arches striding over the new-born stream,
The village glittering in the noontide beam.

Poetic ardours in my bosom swell,
Lone wandering by the hermit's mossy cell;
The sweeping theatre of hanging woods,
The incessant roar of headlong tumbling floods –
Here Poesy might wake her heaven-taught lyre,
And look through Nature with creative fire;
Here, to the wrongs of Fate half reconciled,
Misfortune's lightened steps might wander wild;
And Disappointment, in these lonely bounds,
Find balm to soothe her bitter rankling wounds;
Here heart-struck Grief might heavenward stretch her scan,
And injur'd Worth forget and pardon man.

One Night as I did Wander

One night as I did wander,
When corn begins to shoot,
I sat me down to ponder
Upon an old tree-root:
Old Ayr ran by before me,
And hastened to the seas;
A wild pigeon cooed over me,
That echoed through the trees.

Again Rejoicing Nature

Chorus
And must I still on Menie dote,
And bear the scorn that is in her eye?
For it is jet, jet-black, and it is like a hawk,
And it will not let a body be.

Again rejoicing Nature sees
Her robe assume its vernal hues:
Her leafy locks wave in the breeze,
All freshly steeped in morning dews.

In vain to me the cowslips blow,
In vain to me the violets spring;
In vain to me in glen or woods,
The mavis and the linnet sing.

The merry plough-boy cheers his team,
With joy the careful seeds-man stalks;
But life to me is a weary dream,
A dream of one that never wakes.

The wanton coot the water skims,
Among the reeds the duckling cry,
The stately swan majestic swims,
And every thing is blessed but I.

The sheep-herd shuts his fold-gate,
And over the moorlands whistles shrill;
With wild, unequal, wandering step,
I meet him on the dewy hill.

And when the lark, between light and dark,
 Blithe awakens by the daisy's side,
And mounts and sings on flittering wings,
 A woe-worn ghost I homeward glide.

Come winter, with your angry howl,
 And raging, bend the naked tree;
Your gloom will soothe my cheerless soul,
 When nature all is sad like me!

I Dreamed I Lay

I dreamed I lay where flowers were springing
    Gaily in the sunny beam,
  Listening to the wild birds singing,
    By a falling crystal stream;
Straight the sky grew black and daring,
Through the woods the whirlwinds rave,
  Trees with aged arms were warring
    Over the swelling, turbid wave.

  Such was my life's deceitful morning,
    Such the pleasures I enjoyed!
But long ere noon loud tempests, storming,
    All my flowery bliss destroyed.
  Though fickle Fortune has deceived me
(She promised fair, and performed but ill),
  Of many a joy and hope bereaved me,
    I bear a heart shall support me still.

Phillis the Fair

While larks with little wing
Fanned the pure air,
Viewing the breathing Spring,
Forth I did fare.
Gay, the sun's golden eye
Peeped over the mountains high;
'Such your bloom,' did I say –
'Phillis the fair!'

In each bird's careless song,
Glad I did share;
While yonder wild flowers among,
Chance led me there.
Sweet to the opening day,
Rosebuds bent the dewy spray;
'Such your bloom,' did I say –
'Phillis the fair!'

Down in a shady walk
Doves cooing were;
I marked the cruel hawk
Caught in a snare.
So kind may Fortune be!
Such make his destiny,
He who would injure you,
Phillis the fair!

The Meadow-Ridge

When over the hill the eastern star
Tells folding time is near, my sweetheart,
And oxen from the furrowed field
Return so dull and weary, O,
Down by the brook, where scented birches
With dew are hanging clear, my sweetheart,
I will meet you on the meadow-ridge,
My own kind dear, O.

At midnight hour in darkest glen
I would rove, and never be frightened, O,
If through that glen I went to you,
My own kind dear, O!
Although the night were never so wild,
And I were never so weary, O,
I will meet you on the meadow-ridge,
My own kind dear, O.

The hunter loves the morning sun
To rouse the mountain deer, my sweetheart;
At noon the fisher takes to the glen
Down the brook to rouse, my sweetheart:
Give me the hour of twilight grey –
It makes my heart so cheery, O,
To meet you on the meadow-ridge,
My own kind dear, O.

Where Are the Joys

Where are the joys I have met in the morning,
    That danced to the lark's early song?
Where is the peace that awaited my wandering
    At evening the wild-woods among?

No more a-winding the course of yonder river
    And marking sweet flowerets so fair,
No more I trace the light footsteps of Pleasure,
    But Sorrow and sad-sighing Care.

Is it that Summer has forsaken our valleys,
    And grim, surly Winter is near?
No, no, the bees humming round the gay roses
    Proclaim it the pride of the year.

Fondly would I hide what I fear to discover,
    Yet long, long, too well have I known:
All that has caused the wreck in my bosom
    Is Jenny, fair Jenny alone!

Time cannot aid me, my griefs are immortal,
    Not Hope dare a comfort bestow.
Come then, enamoured and fond of my anguish,
    Enjoyment I will seek in my woe!

O Caledonia

A Fiddler in the North

Amang the trees, where humming bees,
At buds and flowers were hinging, O,
Auld Caledon drew out her drone,
And to her pipe was singing, O:
'Twas Pibroch, Sang, Strathspeys, and Reels,
She dirl'd them aff fu' clearly, O:
When there cam' a yell o' foreign squeels,
That dang her tapsalteerie, O.

Their capon craws an' queer "ha, ha's,"
They made our lugs grow eerie, O;
The hungry bike did scrape and fyke,
Till we were wae and weary, O:
But a royal ghaist, wha ance was cas'd,
A prisoner, aughteen year awa',
He fir'd a Fiddler in the North,
That dang them tapsalteerie, O.

As I Stood by Yon Roofless Tower

As I stood by yonder roofless tower,
Where the wallflower scents the dewy air,
Where the owl mourns in her ivy bower,
And tells the midnight moon her care:

Chorus
A girl all alone was making her moan,
Lamenting our lads beyond the sea:–
'In the bloody wars they fall, and our honour is gone and all,
And broken-hearted we must die.'

The winds were laid, the air was still,
The stars they shot along the sky,
The fox was howling on the hill,
And the distant-echoing glens reply.

The stream, down its hazily path,
Was rushing by the ruined wall,
Hurrying to join the sweeping river Nith,
Whose roarings seemed to rise and fall.

The cold blue North was streaming forth
Her lights, with hissing, eerie din:
Athwart the horizon they start and shift,
Like Fortune's favours, lost as soon as won.

Now, looking over firth and fold,
Her horn the pale-faced Cynthia reared,
When lo! in form of minstrel old
A stern and stalwart ghost appeared.

And from his harp such strains did flow,
Might have roused the slumbering Dead to hear,
But O, it was a tale of woe
As ever met a Briton's ear!

He sang with joy his former day,
He, weeping, wailed his latter times:
But what he said – it was no play! –
I will not venture it in my rhymes.

O, Dear Is Me
on My Spinning-Wheel

O, dear is me on my spinning-wheel!
And dear is me on my distaff and reel,
From top to toe that clothes me well,
And wraps me cosy and warm at evening!
I will set me down, and sing and spin,
While low descends the summer sun,
Blessed with content, and milk and meal –
O, dear is me on my spinning-wheel!

On each hand the streamlets trot,
And meet below my thatched cottage,
The scented birch and hawthorn white
Across the pool their arms unite,
Alike to screen the bird's nest
And little fishes' cooler rest.
The sun glances kindly in the shelter,
Where blithe I turn my spinning-wheel.

On lofty oaks the wild pigeons wail,
And Echo cons the doleful tale.
The linnets in the hazel slopes,
Delighted, rival each other's lays.
The corncrake among the clover hay,
The partridge whirring over the meadow,
The swallow darting round my cottage,
Amuse me at my spinning-wheel.

With little to sell and less to buy,
Above distress, below envy,
O, who would leave this humble state
For all the pride of all the great?
Amid their flaring, idle toys,
Amid their cumbrous, noisy joys,
Can they the peace and pleasure feel
Of Bessy at her spinning-wheel?

Castle Gordon

Streams that glide in Orient Plains,
Never bound by Winter's chains;
Glowing here on golden sands,
There intermixed with foulest stains
From tyranny's empurpled hands;
These, their richly gleaming waves,
I leave to tyrants and their slaves:
Give me the stream that sweetly laves
The banks by Castle Gordon.

Spicy forests ever gay,
Shading from the burning ray
Hapless wretches sold to toil;
Or, the ruthless native's way,
Bent on slaughter, blood and spoil;
Woods that ever verdant wave,
I leave the tyrant and the slave:
Give me the groves that lofty brave
The storms of Castle Gordon.

Wildly here without control
Nature reigns, and rules the whole;
In the sober pensive mood,
Dearest to the feeling soul,
She plants the forest, pours the flood.
Life's poor day I will, musing, rave,
And find at night a sheltering cave,
Where waters flow and wild woods wave
By lovely Castle Gordon.

Eli River Banks and Eli Hillsides

O, Eli river banks and Eli hillsides
It was but once I saw you
But all my days I will sing your praise
Who ever may miscall you.
Your trees were in their freshest bloom,
Your birds were singing cheery
When through your waving yellow broom
I wandered with my dear!

How sweet the silver morning sped
In cheerful contemplation!
How fast the golden gloaming fled
In loving conversation!
How down the bank and up the slope
How could I ever weary
In such a place on such a day
With such a lovely dear!

O, Eli river banks and Eli hillsides
Always pleasant be your waters!
May all your sons have winning ways,
And lovely be your daughters!
My life to me must surely be
Existence dull and dreary
If I forget the day we met
When I was with my dear!

Their Groves
of Sweet Myrtle

Their groves of sweet myrtle let foreign lands reckon,
Where bright-beaming summers exalt the perfume!
Far dearer to me yonder lone glen of green bracken,
With the stream stealing under the long, yellow broom;
Far dearer to me are yonder humble broom bowers,
Where the blue-bell and wild daisy lurk lowly, unseen;
For there, lightly tripping among the wild flowers,
Listening to the linnet, often wanders my Jean.

Though rich is the breeze in their gay, sunny valleys,
And cold Caledonia's blast on the wave,
Their sweet-scented woodlands that skirt the proud palace,
What are they? – The haunt of the tyrant and slave!
The slave's spicy forests and gold-bubbling fountains
The brave Caledonian views with disdain:
He wanders as free as the winds of his mountains,
Save Love's willing fetters – the chains of his Jean.

Nature's Law

Humbly Inscribed to Gavin Hamilton, Esquire.

Let other heroes boast their scars,
The marks of struggle and strife,
But other poets sing of wars,
The plagues of human life!
Shame befall the fun: with sword and gun
To slap mankind like lumber!
I sing his name and nobler fame
Who multiplies our number.

Great Nature spoke, with air benign:–
'Go on, you human race;
This lower world I you resign;
Be fruitful and increase.
The liquid fire of strong desire,
I have poured it in each bosom;
Here on this hand does Mankind stand,
And there, is Beauty's blossom!'

The Hero of these artless strains,
A lowly Bard was he,
Who sung his rhymes in Coila's plains
With much mirth and glee:
Kind Nature's care had given his share
Large of the flaming current;
And, all devout, he never sought
To stem the sacred torrent.

...

He felt the powerful, high behest
Thrill vital through and through;
And sought a correspondent breast
To give obedience due.
Propitious Powers screened the young flowers
From mildews of abortion;
And lo! the Bard – a great reward –
Has got a double portion!

Old jolly Coil may count the day,
As annual it returns,
The third of Libra's equal sway,
That gave another Burns,
With future rhymes and other times
To emulate his sire,
To sing old Coil in nobler style
With more poetic fire!

You Powers of peace and peaceful song,
Look down with gracious eyes,
And bless old Coila large and long
With multiplying joys!
Long may she stand to prop the land,
The flower of ancient nations,
And Burnses spring her fame to sing
To endless generations!

Sketch

Hail, Poesy! you nymph reserved!
In chase of you, what crowds have swerved
From Common Sense, or sunk ennerved
    Among heaps of nonsense;
And Och! over often your sweethearts have starved
    Amid all your favours!

Say, Lass why your train among,
While loud the trumpet's heroic clang,
And Sock and buskin spank along
    To death or marriage;
Scarce one has tried the Shepherd-song
    But with miscarriage?

In Homer's craft John Milton thrives;
Eschylus' pen William Shakespeare drives;
Little Pope, the dwarf, still him tugs
    Horatian fame;
In your sweet song, Barauld, survives
    Even Sappho's flame.

But you, Theocritus, who matches?
They are not Herd's ballads, Maro's catches;
Squire Pope but prepares his small patches
    Of Heathen tatters:
I pass by hundreds, nameless wretches,
    That ape their betters.

...

In this great age of wit and learning,
Will none the Shepherd's whistle more
Blow sweetly in its native air
And rural grace;
And with the far-famed Grecian share
A rival place?

Yes! there is one, – a Scottish youth!
There is one: come forward, honest Allan!
You need not cower behind the youth,
A fellow so clever;
The teeth of Time may gnaw Tatallan,
But you are for ever.

You paint old Nature to the nines,
In your sweet Caledonian lines;
No golden stream through myrtles twines
Where Philomel,
While midnight gales rustle clustering vines,
Her griefs will tell!

Your rural loves are Nature's self;
No bombast floods of nonsense swell;
No snap conceits, but that sweet spell
Of witching love,
That charm that can the strongest quell,
The sternest move.

In daisied glens your brooklet stray,
Where lovely girls bleach their clothes;
Or trots by hazel woods and slopes
With hawthorns grey,
Where blackbirds join the shepherd's lays
At close of day.

From:
To William Simpson
of Ochiltree

Old Coila, now, may tingle with delight,
　　She has gotten poets of her own;
Comrades who their chanters would not spare,
　　　　But tune their lays,
　　　Till echoes all resound again
　　　　　Her well-sung praise.

No Poet thought her worth his while,
　　To set her name in measured style;
　She lay like some unknown-of isle
　　　　Beside New Holland,
　Or where wild-meeting oceans boil
　　　　South of Magellan.

Ramsay and famous Fergusson
　Gave Forth and Tay a lift above;
Yarrow and Tweed, to many a tune,
　　　Over Scotland rings;
While Irwin, Lugar, Aye, and Doon
　　　　Nobody sings.

The Illissus, Tiber, Thames, and Seine,
Glide sweet in many a tuneful line:
But, Willie, set your foot in mine,
　　　And cock your crest!
We will make our streams and brooklets shine
　　　　Up with the best.

...

We will sing old Coila's plains and hills,
Her moors red-brown with heather bells,
Her banks and slopes, her dens and dells,
    Where glorious Wallace
All bore the highest honours, as stories tell,
    From Southern fellows.

At Wallace' name, what Scottish blood
But boils up in a spring-tide flood?
Often have our fearless fathers strode
    By Wallace' side,
Still pressing onward, red-wet-shod,
    Or gloriously died!

O, sweet are Coila's hollows and woods,
When linnets chant among the buds,
And sporting hares, in amorous gambols,
    Their loves enjoy;
While through the hillsides the wild pigeon coos
    With wailing cry!

Even winter bleak has charms to me,
When winds rave through the naked tree;
Or frosts on hills of Ochiltree
    Are hoary grey;
Or blinding drifts wild-furious flee,
    Darkening the day!

O Nature! all your shows and forms
To feeling, pensive hearts have charms!
Whether the summer kindly warms,
    With life and light;
Or winter howls, in gusty storms,
    The long, dark night!

Yonder Wild
Mossy Mountain

Yonder wild mossy mountains so lofty and wide,
That nurse in their bosom the youth of the Clyde,
Where the grouse lead their coveys through heather to feed,
And the shepherd tends his flock as he pipes on his reed.

Not Gowrie's rich valley nor Forth's sunny shores
To me have the charms of yonder wild, mossy moors;
For there, by a lonely, sequestered stream,
Resides a sweet girl, my thought and my dream.

Among those wild mountains shall still be my path,
Each stream foaming down its own green, narrow valley;
For there with my girl the long day I wander,
While over us unheeded fly the swift hours of love.

She is not the fairest, although she is fair;
Of nice education but small is her share;
Her parentage humble as humble can be;
But I love the dear lassie because she loves me.

To Beauty what man but must yield him a prize,
In her armour of glances, and blushes, and sighs?
And when Wit and Refinement has polished her darts,
They dazzle our eyes, as they fly to our hearts.

But kindness, sweet kindness, in the fond sparkling eye
Has lustre outshining the diamond to me,
And the heart beating love as I am clasped in her arms,
O, these are my girl's all-conquering charms!

My Heart's
in the Highlands

My heart is in the Highlands, my heart is not here,
My heart is in the Highlands a-chasing the deer,
A-chasing the wild deer and following the roe –
My heart is in the Highlands, wherever I go!

Farewell to the Highlands, farewell to the North,
The birthplace of valour, the country of worth!
Wherever I wander, wherever I rove,
The hills of the Highlands for ever I love.

Farewell to the mountains high covered with snow,
Farewell to the broad valleys and green valleys below,
Farewell to the forests and wild-hanging woods,
Farewell to the torrents and loud-pouring floods!

Paraphrase of
the First Psalm

The man in life wherever placed,
Has happiness in store,
Who walks not in the wicked's way
Nor learns their guilty lore;

Nor from the seat of scornful pride
Casts forth his eyes abroad,
But with humility and awe
Still walks before his God!

That man shall flourish like the trees,
Which by the streamlets grow:
The fruitful top is spread on high,
And firm the roots below.

But he, whose blossom buds in guilt,
Shall to the ground be cast,
And, like the rootless stubble, tossed
Before the sweeping blast.

For why? that God the good adore
Has given them peace and rest,
But has decreed that wicked men
Shall never be truly blessed.

Glossary and Gazetteer

Aberfeldie	Aberfeldy, a market town in Highland Perthshire
Afton	river in Ayrshire
Albion	here a poetical name for Scotland, historically occasionally called Albany and called in Gaelic Alba
ald	old
Athole	Atholl, ancient Highlands region of north-central Scotland
Ayr	coastal town and royal burgh in Ayrshire; also the name of the longest river in Ayrshire
Ayrshire	historic county of south-west Scotland
Ballochmyle	landed estate and house near Catrine in East Ayrshire
Ben Ledi	mountain in Stirlingshire
bonny	pretty, attractive
Borealis	Aurora Borealis – the Northern Lights
Boreas	god of the north wind in classical mythology associated with the winter cold
brake	thicket
Breadalbane	region of south-central Highlands
Bruar Water	river in Perthshire famous for its waterfalls and scenic beauty, though Burns thought it needed to be planted with more trees and thicket
bushel	traditional dry or liquid measure in Britain roughly equal to 8 imperial gallons or 4 pecks
Caledonia	poetical name for Scotland derived from the Latin name for the Highlands or, more generally, northern Britain
Castle Gordon	country house and estate in Moray, seat of the dukes of Gordon
Catrine	village in East Ayrshire
Cessnock Water	river of East Ayrshire
Clyde	major river of Scotland that runs into the Firth of Clyde

Coil	Coel Hen, Pictish king of south-west Scotland who gave his name to a district covering much of Ayrshire (Kyle); Burns also personified the area as his (female) muse, Coila.
Corsencon	hill and landmark in Ayrshire
cot	cottage
cotter/cottar	a farm labourer living as a tenant in a cottage
Craigieburn	estate near Moffat in Dumfriesshire
Cree	river in south-west Scotland flowing into the Solway Firth
Cummins	John Comyn III of Badenoch (c. 1274–1306), Scottish baron known as the Red Comyn and rival to Robert the Bruce for the throne
Cynthia	name for Artemis, as moon goddess, and the moon itself
deil	the Devil
Devon	tributary of the Forth flowing down from the southern Highlands
Doon	river in Ayrshire
driech	dreary weather
Dryburgh	hamlet next to the River Tweed and site of a ruined abbey
Dunse	Duns, market town in Berwickshire, south-east Scotland
Eden Water	tributary of the River Tweed in south-east Scotland
Ednam	village in Roxburghshire, just outside Kelso
Eolian	produced by the wind, derived from Aeolus, god of the winds in classical mythology
Forth	major river of Central Scotland running into the North Sea via the Firth of Forth and Edinburgh
Gowrie	ancient region of central Scotland
handsel	a new year's gift for good luck
Hamilton, Gavin	Scottish Neoclassical painter (1723–98)
Helicon	a mountain scared to the muses; a spring found on the mountain, Hippocrene, was a byword for poetic inspiration
Herd, David	Scottish collector of ballads (1732–1810)
John Barleycorn	personification of barley as well as whisky, one of the drinks made from the grain
Kenmore	village in Perthshire

kirk	church
Lammas	festival marking the first harvest of the season, held on 1 August
lave, to	to wash
lea	meadow
Logan Water	river of south-west Scotland
Magellan, Strait of	narrow strait on the southern tip of South America, between Chile and Tierra del Fuego, and an important sea route between the Atlantic and Pacific
Martinmas	St Martin's Day (11 November), often celebrated with feasting and merrymaking marking the end of harvest and the beginning of winter
mavis	song thrush
New Holland	name given to Australia by Europeans from the 17th century
Nith	a river in south-west Scotland
Ochiltree	village in Ayrshire
Parnassus	mountain in Greece sacred to Apollo and the Muses
peck	traditional dry or liquid measure in Britain roughly equal to 2 imperial gallons
Philomel	poetic name for the nightingale, from a Greek heroine who was turned into this bird
Phoebus	name for Apollo, the god of the sun in classical mythology
Theocritus	ancient Greek poet (born c. 300 BCE) considered the father of pastoral poetry
Thomson, James	Scottish poet (1700–48) born in Ednam, Roxburghshire, author of the influential sequence *The Seasons* (1730)
throe	suffering
Tweed	the most important river in south-east Scotland
Wallace, William	Scottish nobleman (died 1305) and national hero who helped lead the Scots to victory at the Battle of Stirling Bridge (1297)
warp	weave
Yarrow Water	river in south-west Scotland, a tributary of Ettrickwater, which in turn is a tributary of the Tweed